D0535269

DATE DUE

FEB 07 '95	
DEC 10 '96	

Gangs

Look for these and other books in the Lucent
Overview series:

Abortion
Acid Rain
AIDS
Alcoholism
Animal Rights
The Beginning of Writing
Cancer
Dealing with Death
Death Penalty
Drugs and Sports
Drug Trafficking
Eating Disorders
Endangered Species
Energy Alternatives
Extraterrestrial Life
Gangs
Garbage
Greenhouse Effect
Gun Control
Hazardous Waste
The Holocaust
Homeless Children
Ocean Pollution
Oil Spills
The Olympic Games
Ozone
Population
Rainforests
Recycling
Smoking
Special Effects in the Movies
Teen Alcoholism
Teen Pregnancy
The UFO Challenge
Vietnam

Gangs

by Karen Osman

LUCENT
B·O·O·K·S

LUCENT Overview Series

LUCENT *Overview Series*

Library of Congress Cataloging-in-Publication Data

Osman, Karen, 1955-
    Gangs / by Karen Osman.
        p.   cm. — (Lucent overview series)
    Includes bibliographical references and index.
    Summary: Discusses the history of gangs in the United States,
describing current characteristics of gangs, and presenting
consequences of and solutions to gang activity.
    ISBN 1-56006-131-6 (alk. paper)
    1. Gangs—United States—History—Juvenile literature.
[1. Gangs.]   I. Title.   II. Series.
HV6439.U5086   1992
364.1'066'0973—dc20   92-28009
                                                              CIP
                                                               AC

*This book is lovingly
dedicated to my parents,
Samuel and Virginia*

Acknowledgments

The author would like to gratefully acknowledge the help of Ron Lopez, chairman of the Department of Behavior and Social Sciences at Los Angeles Southwest College; Robert Ferber of the gang unit of the Los Angeles city attorney's office; James Diego Vigil, associate professor of anthropology, University of Southern California; Ron Chance of the University of Chicago National Youth Gang Project; Thomas C. Mackey, assistant professor of history, University of Louisville; and Arthur Andrew Lopez, Esq., friend and adviser.

Contents

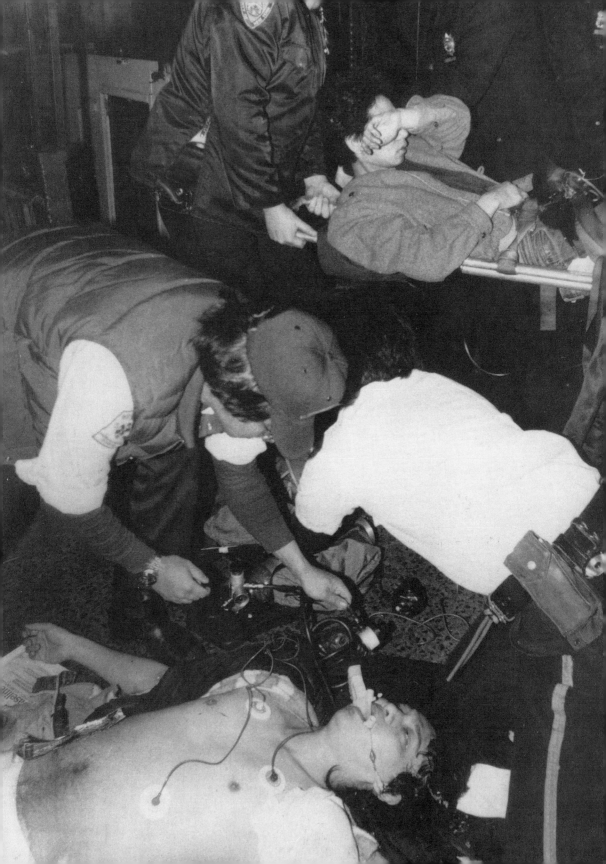

Introduction

ALL ACROSS THE United States, gangs, and the problems they create, are increasing. Armed with handguns, assault rifles, and semi-automatic pistols, gang members are lashing out against society in frustration and anger. Entire neighborhoods have become battle zones. Sucked into a life-style in which they must kill or be killed, young people die every day on American streets.

"They're killing each other, and it's getting worse all the time," said writer Leon Bing. "Their lives are so desolate, they have so little hope, and they are taking it out on people like themselves."

In the last ten years, more than thirty-five hundred people have died in gang violence in Los Angeles alone. In Chicago, 11 percent of all the homicides in 1990 were gang-related. Small and midsize cities that have never had gang problems before are reporting gang-associated drug trafficking, vandalism, and murders.

Gang members are not the only ones affected by this escalating violence. In some areas, as many as one-half of all gang-related murder victims are innocent bystanders caught in the cross fire. Those who are not killed or injured experience grief, fear, and intimidation.

(Opposite page) Paramedics fight to save the lives of two men injured in a battle between rival gangs.

"Gangs hold many neighborhoods hostage," the federal *Juvenile Justice Bulletin* reports.

9

Residents are fearful of leaving their homes. They are afraid to let their children play in area parks that have been taken over by gangs for drug dealing. Neighborhood businesses suffer economically because residents are hesitant to leave their homes to shop. And community services, such as law enforcement and courts, find themselves with escalating costs as they struggle to deal with gangs.

Gangs are one result of the poverty, discrimination, and urban deterioration that threaten the United States today. Some experts say that young people, undereducated and without access to good jobs, become frustrated with their lives and join gangs as an alternative to boredom, hopelessness, and devastating poverty.

"I have seen eight-year-old girls alone by the roadside holding up signs reading I WILL WORK FOR FOOD," one writer said. "What do you think is going to happen to them? All the

Sheriff's deputies handcuff suspected gang members in Los Angeles.

time, homeless children turn up in gang neighborhoods knocking on doors, saying, 'I want to claim. I want to be from this "hood".' And the gangs let them in."

Though there are gangs in many communities, the hardest hit are America's poor and segregated slums and ghettos, where frustration levels are already high. Gangs add to the problems. As death counts rise, people search desperately for ways to combat the violence and struggle to survive in gang-infested communities. With protective bars on their doors and windows, citizens are afraid to let their children play outdoors and are afraid themselves to walk down the street after sundown.

Study after study has tried to determine why gangs plague some communities, but researchers, too, are frustrated. There is no one accepted theory that explains why gangs form and why they do what they do. As a result, people working to solve the communities' gang problems have difficulty. They find themselves overwhelmed, armed with little more than outdated theories and their own intuition.

So the violence continues. Lives are wasted every day in a world of flying bullets and gripping poverty.

1

The History of Street Gangs in the United States

STREET GANGS HAVE existed in the United States since at least the late eighteenth century. Though most of these gangs are not directly related to the gangs of today, the various groups have had much in common. Many of the rites, rituals, and activities associated with today's gangs had their beginnings in these early gangs. Many of the same social conditions caused their formation.

Over the centuries, with few exceptions, the ingredients for gang formation have been poverty, discrimination, and hopelessness. For the most part, gangs have appeared in the poorest sections of cities. Usually, gang members are of the same race, and the group is seen as a means of protection, recreation, or financial gain.

The eighteenth century

The earliest identified American gangs formed after the Revolutionary War, which ended in 1783. They were the Smith's Vly gang, the Bowery Boys, the Broadway Boys, the Fly Boys, and the Long Bridge Boys. The Smith's Vly, the

(Opposite page) Early gangs often consisted of youths in their early teens. Fighting was their primary activity.

13

Poverty often forced immigrants to settle in city slums. With little hope for the future, some of these young people turned to gangs.

Bowery Boys, and the Broadway Boys were white gangs. The Fly Boys and the Long Bridge Boys were African-American.

Members were in their early teens and twenties, and not all came from the poorest classes. Many worked as carpenters, butchers, and mechanics, for example. Unlike many gangs that followed, their members were not necessarily criminals who committed violent crimes or murdered rivals. They did fight, however. It was not unusual for tradespeople to claim and defend their territory during this period.

It was not until the nineteenth century that criminal gangs first formed. As the result of a worsening economy and a growing population that increased the competition for jobs, gangs began to specialize in crime. These gangs became a part of life in America's growing cities.

Nineteenth-century New York City

Irish immigrants formed the first American criminal gangs in New York City during the early 1800s. They relied on gangs for protection and financial gain when neither could be obtained by other means. Like many immigrants who would later arrive, a good portion of the Irish who came to the United States were poor. Fleeing famine and political oppression in Ireland, they often came to the United States penniless and without friends. Primarily rural people, they were forced by lack of money and weariness to settle in large cities instead of the countryside. The poorest moved into city slums, where there was already overcrowding, disease, and filth.

Many of the poorest Irish settled in the Five Points area of New York, which was one of the nation's most notorious slums. In Five Points, the Irish gangs organized, appointed leaders, and chose gang names. They had dress codes—the

Roach Guards wore blue stripes and the Dead Rabbits wore red stripes—and chose nicknames for their members. Many of the rituals associated with today's gangs have their roots in this period.

The first Irish gang known to have a recognized leader was the Forty Thieves, which was organized by Edward Coleman in 1826. Not much is known about Coleman or his gang. Members were pickpockets, thugs, and thieves. Their victims were usually well-dressed men and law enforcement officers.

At about the same time, other gangs sprang up in the city. Some were criminal gangs, some specialized in brawling, and some were simply made up of members who had the same political views. For example, many Irish gangs came together because of their shared hatred of the British, with whom they had a centuries-old dispute. Others aligned themselves with local political parties. In Five Points, there were the Chichesters, the Roach Guards, the Plug Uglies, the Shirt Tails, and the Dead Rabbits, among others. There were

Youthful members of an early-American gang. Gangs often formed where poverty, discrimination, and hopelessness existed.

A gang member watches as his friends practice their skill at pickpocketing.

also many gangs in an area known as the Bowery. Some of these were the True Blue Americans, the O'Connell Guards, and the Atlantic Guards. The Five Points gang members were mostly poor and unemployed and the Bowery gang members came mostly from the poor working class.

Most of the Bowery gangs were brawling gangs, which specialized in fighting. Gang members carried knives, brickbats, bludgeons, brass knuckles, ice picks, and pikes. Some of them had pistols and muskets. There were even reports of gangs firing cannons.

The Bowery gangs and the Five Points gangs brawled on a regular basis. They fought over turf, or gang territory, and ethnic differences. Sometimes, the battles were so long and so fierce—with muskets and pistols blazing—that the army had to be called in to stop them. When things calmed down between the neighborhoods, gangs within the same community fought each other for sport and over politics.

Recreational violence was common. Gang members thought nothing of injuring or murdering total strangers. One Plug Ugly was reported to have cracked a stranger's spine in three places in order to win a two-dollar bet.

Philadelphia

In Philadelphia, reports of youth gang activity surfaced as early as 1840. David R. Johnson writes in *Policing the Urban Underworld* that between 1840 and 1870, Philadelphia was home to at least one hundred youth gangs. These gangs formed primarily in low-income communities near working-class neighborhoods. Most gang members were between ages ten and nineteen.

Each gang developed its own personality, although sometimes one gang adopted the behavior of another. Generally, the gangs can be grouped into four basic categories—those that hung out on street corners, those that committed theft, those that committed acts of violence, and those that engaged in combat.

Some gangs specialized in certain types of crimes such as theft. Here, boys steal from a merchant's cart.

Street corner gangs were more of a nuisance than a threat. Their activities ranged from prowling the streets to throwing snowballs and rocks at pedestrians. Gangs that specialized in theft were more than a nuisance. They burglarized and vandalized homes, often smashing anything they could not carry away. Violent gangs were a menace. Members did not stay in any single area. They roamed the streets, attacking pedestrians, police officers, young boys, and members of other ethnic or racial groups.

Combat gangs were territorially based. They were attached to and protective of their neighborhoods. Their primary activity was fighting, and they usually fought over territory or ethnic, political, and religious differences.

Territorial fights rarely resulted in serious injuries. They were almost like sports events and usually involved youths from the same community fighting for control of a neighborhood. Gang members would gather in a vacant lot and fight with fists, bricks, and stones. Often, crowds of older men would watch and cheer on their favorite gang.

Fights over culture, beliefs, and race were much worse than territorial fights because they were more emotional, with Irish Catholics usually pitted against Protestants. Many of these fights ended in serious injury and death. Gangs fought over such issues as the outlawing of alcoholic beverages, Bible reading in public schools, and immigrant rights.

After the Civil War

When the Civil War ended in 1865, gangs were still evolving into what they have become today. In New York, records indicate the presence of Jewish gangs, Italian gangs, African-American gangs, and Irish gangs. Chinese gangs appeared

in California in the mid-1800s. During this time, murder became a test of toughness, and drugs became a part of the gang scene.

The Whyos of Five Points were the first gang suspected of using murder as a membership requirement. According to street legend, the Whyos refused to accept a new member unless he had committed, or at least had tried to commit, one murder. Herbert Asbury, in his book *The Gangs of New York*, says this legend may have come from one incident. In 1883, a Whyo named Mike McGloin murdered a man who had caught him stealing. The day after the murder, McGloin was quoted as saying: "A guy ain't tough until he has knocked his man out!" Those who heard the

The late 1800s were a difficult time for many new immigrants. Social reformer Jacob Riis captured the harshness of the streets in this photograph taken in New York City in 1888.

statement took it to mean that in order to be a Whyo, a person had to prove his toughness by killing someone.

Gangs and drugs

It was also during this time that drugs—primarily morphine, laudanum, and cocaine—entered gang life. Laudanum, an opium-based drug, was very popular. It did not require a prescription, and ordinary people took it often for headaches, toothaches, depression, and other ailments. Gangs used laudanum as knockout drops. A gang member would slip an overdose of laudanum into someone's food or drink and that person would pass out. The victim was then an easy target for theft or even murder. Gang members also used this drug to get high themselves.

Morphine, a strong painkiller derived from opium, was also popular with gang members and the public. Cocaine, however, was the most sought-after drug. One historian estimates that 90 percent of one nineteenth-century gang, the Hudson Dusters, used cocaine. It was even rumored that the idea for their name came from cocaine dust.

The Hudson Dusters were, perhaps, one of the most colorful gangs in all of gang history. Founded in the 1890s, this gang was known for its parties. The Dusters entertained such celebrities as playwright Eugene O'Neill, and they were a favorite with journalists, who enjoyed their flashiness as well as their food and drink. Though they did defend their borders, they were relatively peaceful. The gang did not, however, last long.

Author Luc Sante attributes the downfall of the Dusters to their drug habit: "Ultimately, they succumbed to this weakness in one way or another, and were gone from the scene by 1916."

Gang members, by the end of the nineteenth century, also started wearing distinctive jackets. One Lung Curran of the West Side Gophers of New York is credited with starting the fad. Legend has it that One Lung's girlfriend was upset because he did not have a suitable fall coat. To please her, he walked out, hit a policeman over the head, and stole his coat. His girlfriend made the coat into a jacket. The jacket was so admired that other Gophers went out and started doing the same.

A new century of violence

By the early 1900s, gang activity was widespread. Cities in the United States had been growing at a rapid pace. More immigrants were entering the country, and the gap between rich and poor was widening. All across the nation, in every urban area where poor, hopeless people lived, gangs appeared.

Jacob Riis, a social reformer, photographer, and journalist writing at the turn of the century, documented the problems of these areas. In *The Battle with the Slum*, first published in 1902, he writes:

> The slum is as old as civilization. Civilization implies a race to get ahead. In a race there are usually some who for one cause or another cannot keep up, or are thrust out from among their fellows. They fall behind, and when they have been left far in the rear they lose hope and ambition, and give up. Thenceforward, if left to their own resources, they are the victims, not the masters of their environment; and it is a bad master. They drag one another always farther down. The bad environment becomes the heredity of the next generation.

Riis claimed that criminality, immorality, and violence were symptoms of a disease that was the slum itself. He was convinced that if society

Social reformer Jacob Riis captured members of the Short Tail gang huddled under a pier in this 1894 photograph.

Chicano zoot-suiters wave white flags after "surrendering" to police during the 1943 zoot suit riots in Los Angeles.

could eliminate poverty and hopelessness, it could eliminate the associated problems. But slums and their gangs continued to grow all across the United States. Even midwestern cities like Chicago reported gang activity.

By the mid-1920s, there were an estimated 1,313 gangs in Chicago and more than twenty-five thousand gang members. According to Frederick Thrasher in *The Gang*, gang members in the 1920s were young. More than half were between the ages of eleven and twenty-five, but some were as young as six and some as old as fifty. Most members were male. Gang activities ranged from stealing ice cream from girls' parties to participating in race riots.

Gang warfare was widespread. Groups from one area of Chicago would often fight with each other or with groups from other areas. For the most part, gangs fought along ethnic, cultural, or racial lines. Italian and Polish gangs dominated the North Side. The gangs on the West Side were primarily Polish, Italian, African-American, Irish, Jewish, and Lithuanian. To the south, more Italian, African-American, Irish, Polish, and Lithuanian groups prowled the streets. Some gangs had no noticeable cultural, ethnic, or national ties and consisted mostly of whites.

Los Angeles

The 1920s and 1930s saw the rise of Chicano gangs in Los Angeles. A Chicano is an American of Mexican descent, and by the early 1900s, Chicanos had settled in many neighborhoods in the Southwest. Many came from working-class families. They formed gangs for recreation and to protect their neighborhoods from outsiders.

By the 1940s, Chicano gangs had established their place in Los Angeles. The zoot suit riots of 1943 helped solidify their role. In these riots, ethnic tensions exploded. White residents and visiting soldiers harassed and beat up young Chicano men who dressed in the popular zoot suit style of tapered pants; long, wide-shouldered coats; and broad-brimmed hats. The zoot-suiters fought back.

This helped strengthen the gangs. With a common foe, gang members banded together more tightly, and gang activity increased.

Drug use also became a part of the Chicano gang scene in the 1940s when members began using drugs for recreation. The problem started out small but quickly grew. For example, in the White

A smiling zoot-suiter shows off his torn clothes and bruised body after the zoot suit riots.

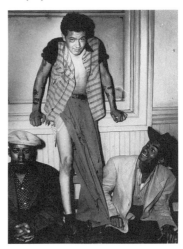

Fence barrio, or neighborhood, in 1947, only one member of the White Fence Gang used heroin. By the early 1950s, there were fifteen drug users. These members started their own subgang, which was made up of drug users and pushers.

The gangs of the 1950s

The 1950s saw the rise of fighting gangs in New York, Philadelphia, Boston, Chicago, Detroit, and Cleveland. Gangs with colorful names like the Dragons, the Mau Maus, the Gowanus, the Tigers, and the Enchanters roamed the city streets, fighting each other, committing crimes, and getting into trouble.

Members of these gangs were usually in their teens. Their gangs had an organized structure, and their primary activity was fighting. Leaders had titles, such as president, captain, warlord, and lieutenant. These gangs had their own special codes of dress—black leather jackets were very popular—and ways of talking and walking. Body language said a lot about the nature of a gang.

James Haskins in his book *Street Gangs Yesterday and Today* says:

> There were ways to tell fighting gangs from non-fighting gangs. When a gang decided to become a fighting or 'bopping' gang, its members immediately took on a different way of walking. A rhythmic gait, characterized by the forward movement of the head with each step, this walk was immediately recognizable.

In New York, as in other big cities, street fighting was at an all-time high. Gang members had guns, knives, and homemade weapons, and they used them frequently. "Bopping," "rumbling," and "jitterbugging" were all terms for street fighting, which was their way of life. Gang members were often seriously injured or killed in their rumbles.

The gangs in New York usually formed and

Gangs in the 1950s showed unity through their dress. Black leather jackets were popular attire for some gangs.

fought along racial lines. They were, for the most part, African-American, white, or Puerto Rican, and they usually fought over girls or turf.

Turf could range from a few blocks to many blocks. It was guarded jealously. A lone boy or a small group of boys from one gang could be beaten simply because they had entered another gang's turf. This, in turn, could be the cause of a full-scale rumble.

Gang members also protected the honor of their girlfriends. "Often a girl was the reason a gang war started. An improper glance from a member of another gang could touch off a battle over her honor or love," says Haskins.

Girl gangs, in fact, began to form in the 1950s. No one knows for certain how many girls joined gangs. The New York City Youth Board, an organization formed in 1947 to work with troubled inner-city youths, claimed there were at least six thousand girls in gangs by 1961. Usually, girl gangs had strong ties with boy gangs and adopted a version of the boy gang's name. For example, the Avengers had the Avenger Debs, the Daggers had the Dagger Debs, and so on.

Gang activity appeared to lessen during the 1960s, a decade when many young people embraced the ideals of peace and love, and took part in events such as this "love-in" in Detroit, Michigan.

Girl gang activities ranged from drinking and smoking marijuana to mugging and shoplifting. Like their male counterparts, girl gangs often rumbled. They also carried weapons and drugs for the boys because they were less likely to be searched by police.

By this time, drug use had become common in many areas of New York. The most popular drugs, besides alcohol, were marijuana and heroin. Many gangs did not consider marijuana use a threat. Heroin, however, was another matter. Young men using heroin, gang members reasoned, were unreliable and not very good in a fight. In addition, they could no longer be trusted because an addict's first priority is his drug.

Gang members often urged addicted friends to stop using heroin. If their attempts failed, they would shun the addicts. Drug pushers were often beaten up and run out of New York neighborhoods by gangs. Still, drug problems were increasing.

In order to combat the rise in violence and drug abuse, organizations like the New York City Youth Board sent social workers into the slums to form relationships with the gangs. Once accepted by gang members, these professionals tried to turn fighting gangs into social clubs. In some cases, this worked. There was much debate, however, over the Youth Board's methods and effectiveness. But there is no doubt that during the 1960s, gang activity seemed to decrease.

The silent sixties

In the 1960s, gangs all but disappeared. There are many theories about why this happened. Some people attribute slackened gang activity to better social service programs or police crackdowns. Others suggest that gang activity slowed because members matured or died in fights. Some

even think the disappearance of gangs reflected the times.

This was the decade in which peace, love, and harmony were the ideals. All across the United States, young people banded together to protest racial discrimination and the war in Vietnam. Some people think that gang members simply traded one form of rebellion for another and that they turned from street crime to political protest, joining larger groups of young people who were clamoring for social change.

Other experts think gang activity never really slowed down. They argue that the press just stopped reporting it because there were other, bigger stories.

No matter what the reason, gangs did not *appear* to be a major problem in the 1960s and early 1970s. After that, the problem reemerged with a vengeance.

Protesters demand equality in a 1960s civil rights march in Washington, D.C. The clamor for social change may have temporarily halted gang activity.

2

Gangs Today

IN THE 1990s, gangs have once again become a part of urban life. From Los Angeles to New York, from Miami to Chicago, gang activity is increasing. More young people are joining gangs, and they are committing more violent crimes. Gang arsenals contain handguns, semiautomatic weapons, and, in some cases, bombs. Over the last ten years, more than thirty-five hundred people have died in gang-related violence in Los Angeles alone.

Though gangs have been reported in all fifty states, few people really understand them. However, members of the University of Chicago National Youth Gang Suppression and Intervention Program, also called the National Youth Gang Project, have studied gangs nationwide. This group defines a street gang as

> a group of people that form an allegiance based on various social needs and engage in acts injurious to public health and public morals. Members of street gangs engage in (or have engaged in) gang-focused criminal activity either individually or collectively; they create an atmosphere of fear and intimidation within the community.

(Opposite page) An East Los Angeles gang member proudly throws his gang hand symbol in front of a memorial to slain gang members.

Gang members come from many backgrounds. Some gangs still form in immigrant communities populated, for example, by recent arrivals from Vietnam, El Salvador, and Haiti. Other gangs cul-

29

Drug gangs are spreading from big cities to small cities and rural areas across the country. Los Angeles gangs such as the Crips and Bloods can be found from Seattle to Washington, D.C. Jamaican gangs such as Spangler, Tivoli Gardens, and Waterhouse are represented from Los Angeles to Boston. Miami-based gangs such as the 34th Street Players and the Untouchables have branched into communities throughout Florida, and Chicago gangs such as the Cobras and Latin Kings have spread throughout the Midwest.

tivate members in neighborhoods consisting of families who have lived in the United States for generations.

Gang members are mostly male and usually range in age from thirteen to twenty-four, though some gangs have members as young as eight or as old as forty. Girls also join gangs but usually leave at the end of adolescence.

Gang geography

Although gangs generally are more numerous in large metropolitan areas like Los Angeles, gang activity also occurs in midsize cities like Fort Wayne, Indiana, and in small cities like Benton Harbor, Michigan.

In Los Angeles, New York, and Chicago, gang activity has a long history, and gang membership

The Spread of Powerful Gangs

Los Angeles gangs
Jamaican gangs
Miami gangs
Chicago gangs

Source: Newsweek

is large. In 1984, there were an estimated 450 gangs and 40,000 gang members in Los Angeles County; today, officials estimate there are twice as many gangs and more than 100,000 members. According to the National Youth Gang Project, in 1987 Chicago reported 125 gangs and 12,000 members, and New York reported 66 gangs and 1,780 members. Gangs can also be found in Dallas, Texas; Atlanta, Georgia; Detroit, Michigan, and other large cities.

Midsize cities such as Albuquerque, New Mexico, and Louisville, Kentucky, have also reported gang activity. In 1987, Louisville reported twenty gangs and 1,000 members, and Albuquerque reported forty-eight gangs and 1,575 members. Fort Wayne reported five gangs and 50 members. Benton Harbor, a city of 14,200 people, had approximately twelve gangs with 350 members.

At first glance, these various cities seem to have little in common. They do, indeed, have many differences. Yet they share at least one problem: the presence of gangs on their streets and in their neighborhoods.

Many people have tried to explain why gangs form in certain communities, why young people join them, and why they become more violent every day. No one theory seems to answer all of these questions. But a general picture emerges from interviews and studies conducted by police, sociologists, and other experts. Although generalizations do not address individual needs, hopes, and circumstances, this information can be helpful in understanding who joins gangs and why.

Unchallenging environment

In most cases, gangs form in poor neighborhoods. Residents of these neighborhoods are often socially isolated, separated from the rest of the community by ethnic, cultural, or economic differences. These neighborhoods are usually characterized by overcrowding, high unemployment, high dropout rates, lack of social and recreational services, and a general feeling of hopelessness. These circumstances, experts say, are a big part of what drives many young people into gangs.

Young people who are drawn to gangs typically have a lot of free time. Their neighborhoods often have few organized recreational and social programs, in many cases because money is tight. Unchallenged by their environment, these young people often drift toward gangs merely seeking something to do.

Gangs often fill this gap. Large, sophisticated gangs sometimes have clubhouses with pool tables and video games. Some gangs even sponsor dances and other recreational activities. Other gangs have none of these things but offer members a chance to be with others their own age. Writer Martin Sanchez-Jankowski says:

> The gang provides individuals with entertainment, such as a fraternity does for college students or the Moose and Elk clubs do for their members. Many individuals said they joined the gang because it was the primary social institution of their neighborhood.

In many cases, young people have nothing to do because they have dropped out of school. Inner-city schools with dropout rates of more than 50 percent feed gangs with restless recruits, says Roberto Rivera, director of the anti-gang Chicago Intervention Network. "There's a relationship between kids that leave [school] and [the formation of] gangs. It's an integral part of the process," Rivera told *The American School Board Journal.*

Some experts estimate that more than 80 percent of gang members cannot read or write. Illiterate and uneducated, they find it almost impossible to get a job. As a result, they have even more free time.

Earning a living

Young people who have little hope of finding work sometimes turn to gangs as a means of earning a living. Police and others have documented gang involvement in drug trafficking, illegal weapons sales, robbery, and theft. Some of the more sophisticated gangs take part in running gambling, prostitution, and extortion rings. Extortion is the practice of intimidating people and forcing them to pay money out of fear.

Gang members who engage in this type of illegal activity cannot always count on a steady income, however. They also run the risk of getting caught and serving time in prison. But to some young people—especially those with no education, skills, or job prospects—the promise of occasional income outweighs the risks of getting caught.

At a 1989 National Youth Gang Project conference, a former Chicago gang leader said of his community:

> The economics of the neighborhood was so bad that anybody that was really in desperate need of money and didn't know how to go about making money any other way was drawn right into [the gang] like a vacuum.

Protection

The need for protection also draws some young people into gangs. A gang can offer protection from everyday threats. In some communities, gang members themselves represent everyday threats. Young people who are not in gangs are sometimes beaten or harassed by gang members. To protect themselves from such treatment,

A police officer questions a suspected gang member. To some gang members, the money earned from illegal activity is worth the risk of arrest.

Young people without jobs sometimes turn to gangs to earn a living. Members of the Grape Street gang, one of whom wears his gang's purple bandanna, flash gang signs and money.

they join the gang. "That's how it is on my street—ain't nothin' but gangbangin', you can't get out of it. They gonna want you to claim, and they gonna beat you up if you don't," one young person told writer Leon Bing.

In high-crime neighborhoods, drug pushers, pimps, and thieves represent another threat. A gang can offer protection here, too. A sixteen-year-old from Los Angeles says:

> Man, I joined the Fultons because there are a lot of people out there who are trying to get you and if you don't got protection you in trouble sometimes. My homeboys [fellow gang members] give me protection, so hey, they were the thing to do.

Respect

Some youths see joining a gang as a way to gain the respect they lack at home and in the community. In some neighborhoods, gang members are seen as tough and in control. At the Na-

tional Youth Gang Project conference, a partici-
pant said:

> I was on a power trip. That's why I wanted to get
> into it. I seen all the things the authority people
> got, the respect from the neighbors, the respect
> from your home. That's what I really wanted, I
> guess. Really I wanted to be respected and well-
> known among my peers and that's what influ-
> enced me most.

Gang membership can appeal to a person's
pride. In neighborhoods where gangs have been a
part of the community for years, many young
people see gang members as protectors of the
community. Sanchez-Jankowski says: "They feel
that their families and communities expect them
to join because community members see the gang
as an aid to them and an individual who joins as
meeting his neighborhood obligation."

Young people may also join gangs because all
their friends are doing it. Gangs, in many cases,
grow out of groups of boys or girls who play together as children. They go to the same school,
live in the same neighborhood, and participate in
the same activities. When some of them join a
gang, it just seems like a natural thing for all of
them to do the same. Several current and former
gang members explained their feelings this way:

> Li'l Monster*: Say we're white and we're rich.
> We're in high school and we been buddies since
> grammar school. And we all decide to go to the
> same *college*. Well, *we* all on the same street, all
> those years, and we all just decide to . . .
>
> Rat-Neck: . . . join the gang.
>
> Tee: What I think is formulating here is that human
> nature wants to be accepted. A human being gives
> less of a damn what he is accepted into. At that
> age—eleven to seventeen—all kids want to belong.

Those who do not want to join are often ha-

*Author's note: Many gang and gang members' names
have been changed to maintain anonymity.*

rassed by gang members until they do. Sometimes, the pressure to join can be intense and escalate beyond urging. One California gang member told cultural anthropologist James Diego Vigil:

> I started getting hassled [by gang members] about the way I dressed, the way my hair was cut, who I hung around with, the whole thing, man! About five of them jumped me . . . they wanted me in their gang, man! Anyhow, this kind of thing went on for a month. I knew I had to decide something, regardless of how good my parents had brought me up or how much they loved me. I was the one getting his head banged around school.

A sense of family

Though not all experts agree, some say young people from deeply troubled homes find substitute families in gangs. Many gang members come from homes that have been disrupted by death, divorce, physical abuse, and substance abuse. "The very fact that a kid is in a gang means that something is missing. . . . So many of them come from abusing backgrounds," says criminal justice expert A.C. Jones.

Abuse, neglect, and loss seem to be common themes in the lives of many young gang members. In a 1991 article on Father Gregory Boyle, a priest who works with gang youths in Los Angeles, writer Celeste Fremon reported:

> Pick three, any three of the gang members that hover around Boyle's door and delve into their family dynamics and the stories will disturb your sleep. There is Bandito, whose father died two years ago of a heroin overdose. There is Smiley whose father is continually drunk and abusive. There is Gato, whose basehead [crack addict] mother sold his only warm jacket to buy another hit.

When families are abusive or fall apart, many experts say that young people turn to gangs for the closeness, caring, and love they lack at home. "The gang becomes a family. They are great at communicating with each other. There is trust and respect," says Cynthia Test, who runs an anti-gang program in San Antonio, Texas.

In addition, some experts say that in families where fathers are absent or abusive, young men turn to gangs to find male role models. Tee Rodgers, a social worker and ex-gang member, told an interviewer:

> My mother raised me, true enough. Okay? And she was married. There was a male figure in the house. But I never accepted him as my father. My mother can only teach me so much 'bout being a man-child in the Promised Land. If, after that, there is nothing for me to take pride in, then I enter into manhood . . . backwards, and I stand there, a warrior strong and proud. But there is no outlet for that energy, for me or my brothers, so we *turn on each other*.

Young people from troubled homes sometimes find a sense of family by joining a gang. Pictured here are members of the Grape Street gang.

Gang members who lack structure and direction in their personal lives often find both in a gang. Although gangs vary in structure and direction most operate according to a set of rules and under some kind of leadership. The largest gangs, some with as many as two thousand members, often break into smaller groups. The smaller groups are called clubs and cliques.

Clubs typically bring more territory into a gang. They are really just branches of a larger gang. A club has its own leaders, but they answer to the larger gang. Clubs form so that a gang can expand its territory. This is most common with gangs that sell drugs. Often they move into a new neighborhood by forming a club that will carry on business there.

Cliques bring together gang members of similar ages—especially new, young members—or unite those who share like interests. Some cliques, for example, specialize in burglary or street fighting. Like clubs, cliques are part of a larger gang.

Small groups called sets also form. Sets are basically independent gangs that adopt part of a larger gang's name. They do this primarily because they want to share the larger gang's reputation. In most cases, the sets and the original gang have little or nothing in common. They do not share leaders or loyalty. Often, their only connection is their name.

In the 1970s, many small gangs began changing their names to create an association with the fierce reputation of two Los Angeles gangs, the Crips and the Bloods. The Main Street Gang became the Main Street Crips, and so on. By 1989, law enforcement agencies estimated that two hundred Crips sets and seventy Bloods sets existed in Los Angeles. Some of these sets were thought to have as many as three hundred members. Today, Bloods and Crips sets of varying sizes can be found all across the United States.

Gang structures differ in other ways, too. Many gangs operate informally, more like a group of

Gang members have tried at various times to end the rivalries responsible for gang violence. This 1988 photo shows Bloods member "Twilight" (left) and Crips member "Twelve" (right) during one such publicized effort.

young people just hanging out together. Leadership falls to whoever takes control. Other gangs have distinct leaders who have duties. Highly structured gangs, usually those involved in drug trafficking and other crimes, often have officers who run the gang as if it were a corporation.

This kind of gang might have a president, vice president, and warlord, says writer Martin Sanchez-Jankowski. The president directs the gang's business dealings and keeps gang members in line. The vice president often oversees the gang's communications network, which can include car phones, walkie-talkies, pagers, and beepers. Gang members use these devices to coordinate drug deals and to protect themselves from arrest. They "have their own codes on their pagers, and if their look-out spots what he thinks is police, he just dials up the other guy's pager and puts in a code, so the dealer doesn't do the deal," Capt. Allan Taylor of the Chicago police told the *Chicago Tribune*.

The warlord keeps order at gang meetings, plans fights against rival gangs, and controls the gang arsenal. The warlord often buys the weapons, takes care of them, and distributes them to members.

Highly structured gangs can be found all across the United States, but they are most common in New York, where competition for drug money and status is high. The chain of command ensures that the gang works like a business and helps keep members under control.

The activities of gang members are also controlled or guided by codes of behavior. Though some codes are more formal than others, nearly all gangs abide by the rituals and symbols that have come to be associated with gang life.

3

Rituals and Symbols

MOST GANGS EXIST within a world of intricate ritual and elaborate symbolism. These rituals and symbols guide gang members in life, and in some cases, follow them to their graves.

Many of the symbols of gang life—a jacket, a tattoo, a nickname, a hand sign—contain no particular mystery on their own. But how these symbols are used gives them meaning that few outsiders can understand. These and other symbols set gang members apart from others in the community and enable them to publicly proclaim their loyalty to the gang.

Every ritual in which gang members take part and every symbol they adopt bind them closer to their gang. The identity of the gang becomes the member's identity. Boys known since birth as Jim, Art, or John adopt nicknames like Banger, Shorty, or Curl. Gang members no longer choose styles and colors that suit them. They wear the styles and colors worn by their gang. They are no longer nameless, faceless young people; they are gang members and they walk, talk, and act like gang members.

For gang members who have little else in their lives, a color, a name, and a hand sign can mean a

(Opposite page) A gang member flashes his gang hand sign. The graffiti on the wall behind him commemorates a gang member killed by police officers.

41

great deal. These symbols can become so important that gang members are willing to be shunned, arrested, or beaten to publicly display them. Many gang members are even willing to kill or be killed to protect these potent symbols of identity and respect.

Initiations

One of the most important symbolic acts of any gang member is initiation into the gang. This often involves some kind of physical confrontation. New members frequently are required to prove they can fight without fear.

Gang members refer to this initiation rite as getting "jumped in." The jumping in can be spontaneous, as when gang members run into the initiate on the street and jump him, or it can be planned. In either case, those who stand and fight are in; those who show fear or try to run are out.

Describing his own initiation, one Los Angeles gang member said:

> Two minutes, all the time you fight back anyway you want. If you fall down, it gets longer than two minutes. So you try not to fall. What I did was I fought against the wall. I fought six guys. After it was over, we shook hands. Then, I helped get several other guys in.

For many, this process is a rite of passage. A successful fight leads to peer acceptance, and gang members gain an identity that travels with them wherever they go. New gang members are no longer from "nowhere," a gang term meaning to be without gang affiliation. Gang members feel they can depend on their homeboys, the other members of the gang, and that they belong to a community.

Initiations can be dangerous. "It is not infrequent to find an initiated gang member in a bloody and lacerated [cut up] state, at times with broken bones," a Federal Bureau of Investigation (FBI) bulletin states.

Initiations can also be deadly. Some gangs require new members to prove their courage or loyalty by committing murder or other violent crimes. In a National Youth Gang Project conference, one former Chicago gang member tried to explain gang initiation this way:

> Okay, well initiation is probably going on a hit. I want his head, let me hear him being dead, or we [mess] somebody up who represents something, right. Okay, now that's initiation.

Some initiations are less brutal and more formal. Initiations into some Chinese gangs are among the most formal and ritualized in the United States. Many of these rituals have their origins in the traditions of ancient Chinese societies. For example, in New York, the Ghost Shadows and the Flying Dragons, gangs with seventy

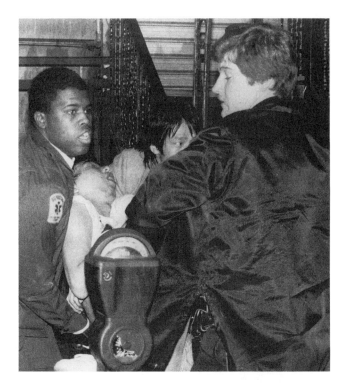

New York City paramedics care for a man who was injured in an attack by the Flying Dragons gang.

to one hundred members each, sometimes require initiates to take an oath, burn yellow paper, and drink wine mixed with drops of blood taken from their fingers.

This kind of initiation promotes solidarity, says writer Ko-Lin Chin. Through this ritual, gang members symbolically become one—they unite into a family.

Colors and tattoos

Initiation is only one of the many rituals of gang life. In many gangs, members are expected to proudly wear the gang's adopted colors and clothing. Today, many gang members wear jackets bearing the name of a professional sports team. For example, in Boston the Greenwood Street Gang wears Green Bay Packers jackets, and the Castlewood Kings wear Cincinnati Reds gear. Some gang members wear particular colors. In Los Angeles, Bloods wear at least one article of red clothing, and Crips wear at least one article of blue. Often this article of clothing is a bandanna. Particular types of athletic shoes are also popular with some gangs. Some Crips, for example, wear the British Knight brand of athletic shoes.

Gang dress is a source of pride for many members. Like a high school athlete's letter sweater, a gang member's shoes, jacket, and colors are symbols of who he is and what he does. Wearing distinctive dress also creates a bond among gang members and symbolizes that they belong.

In some areas of the country, however, gangs have stopped "representing," a gang term that refers to showing outward signs of gang affiliation. Gangs involved in drug trafficking and other illegal activities were among the first to stop wearing identifiable colors and clothing. They prefer to blend in to avoid detection and arrest. Criminologist Carl Taylor explains:

> Detroit kids just laugh when they hear people in L.A. are still wearing colors. . . . What's sweeping this city are what I call CEOS—covert entrepreneurial organizations. They do not wear gold chains or beepers or Fila sweatsuits anymore. They're probably wearing ragged clothes and driving ratty cars.

In addition to distinctive clothing, many gang members have tattoos. This is especially true in Chicano gangs, where members often display tattoos on their arms, hands, or shoulders. Tattoos may be small and simple, like a cross on the hand, or large and detailed. Some of the more ornate gang tattoos cover an entire back or stomach and include the gang member's nickname and gang name.

Tattoos serve several purposes for gang members, says James Vigil. Because of their permanency, tattoos proclaim a lifelong commitment to the gang. They are also respected and envied, especially by neighborhood youngsters who may wish to join the gang someday.

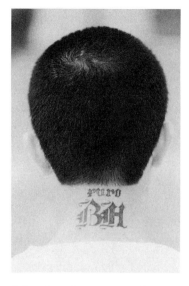

A Los Angeles gang member proclaims his loyalty to his gang by wearing its name tattooed on his neck.

Body language

Just as clothing, colors, and tattoos announce gang affiliation, body language signals a gang member's intentions. Distinctive posture, facial expressions, and gait are as much a part of a gang member's appearance as are shoes and a jacket.

Vigil describes the body language of a typical Chicano gang member:

> Movement is generally methodical, deliberate, and smooth, whether walking out of the front door . . . or sizing up a new group of people with a steady gaze. A walk to the corner, for example, especially when one is alone, will typically be at a leisurely gait, with stiffly postured shoulders and head leaning very slightly back, and eyes fixed forward.

Not only is this body language a form of representing but it can also serve as protection. The gang member looks like someone who is ready for anything. If he is afraid, it can hide his fear. In neighborhoods where crime and violence are a part of life, looking tough can mean the difference between making it to the corner and getting jumped. Most gang members take this body language seriously. Said one former Chicano gang member:

> It's a shame you can't walk down the street with a smile on your face because people take advantage of that. They'll think you soft. You know, you gotta walk around looking like you kill't your mother or something to get your respect.

A misreading of body signals can lead to problems. Some stances, for example, raise a challenge. When some Chicano gang members meet, says Vigil, they often stand an arm's length apart and stare directly at each other. Speaking or stepping away signals a wish not to fight. Taking steps toward the other gang member, however, is as good as accepting the challenge.

Sometimes, just the look in a gang member's eyes can deliver a challenge. Some gangs call this "looking crazy." This look is intended to intimidate another gang member, forcing him to either back off or fight. Writer Bing describes this look:

> He simply narrows his eyes. That's all. He narrows his eyes . . . and everything about his face shifts and changes, as if by some trick of timelapse photography. It becomes a nightmare face, and it is a scary thing to see.

Hand signs

Gang hand signs are another way gang members show their loyalty to their gangs. Each set or gang has its own way of curling or straightening fingers to signal its name. African-American gangs started this practice in Los Angeles, but now many other gangs also have signs.

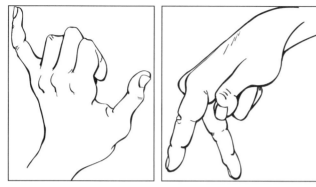

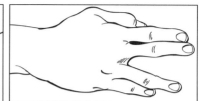

Many gangs have a distinct hand sign. A 1990 National Law Enforcement Institute report identifies some of these signs, including, from left to right, the Neighborhood Bloods, the Avalon Gangster Crips, and the Van Ness Gangster Bloods.

Throwing a hand sign can also serve as a challenge. When two gang members meet, they may make their sign. If the members are from friendly sets, things will probably go smoothly. If they are from warring sets, it is very likely a fight will follow. In some juvenile detention centers where there are a lot of gang members, rules often require inmates to keep their hands in their pockets when in large groups. This keeps them from throwing their sign and starting a fight.

Language

Body language is not the only language of gangs. Over the years, some gangs have developed distinctive written and spoken codes that serve several purposes. Most important, perhaps, they allow private communication in public. Gang writing and speech can be so different from the standard forms that the average person or police officer cannot understand what is being said.

Spoken gang language can differ from gang to gang, or more commonly, from region to region. In some areas of the country, for example, a "dime speed" is a ten-speed bicycle, a person who is "kicking back" is relaxing or killing time, and someone who is "lit up" has been shot. Some Chicano gangs mix slang terms from Spanish and English to create their own language. Among terms commonly used by some Chicano gangs are *vatos*, another word for "guys"; *rifa*, which means "we control"; and *placa*, which refers to graffiti or a graffiti signature.

Graffiti are known to most people as the written language of gangs. Graffiti are the strange, stylized markings scribbled or sprayed on walls, billboards, and street signs in gang-populated communities. Although many gangs use graffiti to mark turf, to challenge other gangs, or to brag about their reputations, communication with graffiti is most highly developed among Chicano gangs.

Graffiti are not meant to be read or understood by the general public. The messages are written by gang members for other gang members. Often, the graffiti contain the writer's nickname, the gang name, and the message itself. A typical

A graffiti-covered wall in a gang-filled neighborhood. Gang graffiti are not meant to be understood by people outside of the gangs.

message, says Vigil, might read: "EL PEGLEG DE 32nd-R-C/S," which would be translated as "I am Pegleg of Thirty-second Street; we're the best and you can't do anything about it."

Graffiti writers make their intentions known by where they write their messages. If a message appears on a building in a gang's home turf, this would confirm the gang's dominance in that area. If, however, the same message appeared in disputed territory—that is, territory over which two gangs are fighting—it would be considered a challenge to the other gang.

Sometimes, rival gang members mark up each other's graffiti. The disfiguring marks can be insults to the original writer or his gang. Also, in some gangs, if a person has been targeted for death, the rival gang will cross his name out. "Line through his name means that person gonna die," one gang member said.

Getting "jumped out"

Most gang members do not stay in gangs all of their life. Some leave for marriage or jobs. Some decide to leave for other reasons. Often, this happens naturally and gradually as the member hangs out with the gang less and less. Sometimes, though, gang members who want to leave are "jumped out," which means they receive a beating. These beatings can be severe. Fifteen-year-old Keith Smith of Waukegan, Illinois, was in a coma for fifty-eight days after being "jumped out" of his gang, for example. Smith's punishment for leaving the gang was supposed to have been a three-minute beating by three gang members. He did not last the full three minutes, however. His attackers were later charged with assault. At a trial for two of the gang members, Smith told the court that he went through with the ritual because he knew he would never be safe if he did not. "They would have caught me somewhere else and beat me up," Smith told the *Chicago Tribune* in 1991.

Some gang members never get the chance to decide whether or not they want to leave their gang because they die of drug overdoses or in gang violence. Though there are no statistics on how many gang members die in these ways, more gang members die young every year as gang activity becomes more violent and drug use rises.

Gang funerals

In some cases, rituals follow gang members to their grave. Caskets are draped with floral arrangements in gang colors with slogans like "We Love You, Homie." T-shirts honoring the dead gang member with messages like "Banger, R.I.P." are common.

Gang members attending the funeral often wear their colors. The dead member is frequently buried in his. The casket is lowered into the ground as gang members wave bandannas and throw their hand sign.

Some gangs bury their dead with modest services and funerals, but others are elaborate. Five hundred friends, relatives, and Crips members

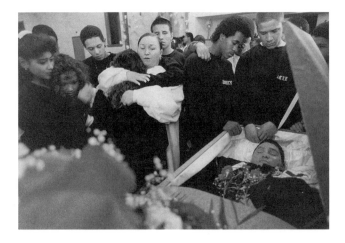

Family and friends gather around a casket to pay their last respects to a dead gang member. Gang members honor the dead by wearing gang colors to the funeral.

Mourners fill the street during the elaborate funeral procession for a longtime gang member known as Cadillac Jim.

gathered in March 1992 at Forest Lawn Memorial Park in Glendale, California, to bury twenty-nine-year-old James Y. Shelton Jr., also known as Cadillac Jim. Shelton had been gunned down one night in front of a cheap motel. *Los Angeles Times* reporters who attended the funeral wrote:

> His deluxe funeral included a silver hearse and four stretch limousines, six floral sprays and other trappings befitting a veteran of more than a decade of gangsterism.
>
> Cadillac Jim's body rested in an open casket underneath an eight-foot banner that bore his name and was fringed with a glistening Crips-blue garland. Many young men, blue scarfs hanging from their back pockets, paused by the casket and had their pictures taken with the body. Some bent to kiss his forehead.

Outside, law enforcement officers stood alert. Police are often necessary because the violence that many times kills gang members sparks again when they are laid to rest. In Los Angeles, rival gang members have stabbed, shot, and stolen corpses. Some have opened fire on the mourners at the funeral home or cemetery. Even the route of a funeral procession is often dictated by gang territory boundaries and a wish to avoid more violence.

4

Crime and Violence

CRIME IS A way of life in many gangs. Armed robbery, theft, extortion, and drug trafficking are common ways for gang members to earn money. Torture, rape, and murder are often regarded as recreation, and committing these crimes is sometimes a way to earn status in the gang.

All across the United States, gang crime and violence are rapidly increasing. In 1990, Los Angeles alone reported 329 gang-related murders; Chicago reported 98. In some large cities, gang murders account for as much as 30 percent of all homicides.

Not all those maimed or murdered are gang members, however. Innocent people are often caught in the cross fire and injured or killed. In some areas, as many as one-half of the victims of all gang murders are innocent bystanders. Their only mistake is being in the wrong place at the wrong time.

"It's like bullets are flying everywhere," Detective Terry Wessel told the *Los Angeles Times* in October 1991. "And where they land, heaven only knows."

In one five-month period in Los Angeles in 1992, for example, five children were hit by gang

(Opposite page) A police officer frisks a suspected gang member for weapons and drugs. Gang-related crime and violence are on the rise across the country.

53

cross fire. According to newspaper accounts, an eleven-year-old girl was hit in the heart by a stray shot as she and her brother waited for an ice-cream truck; a toddler was grazed by a stray bullet while watching television in his parents' apartment; a three-year-old was shot and killed while walking hand in hand with her father; an eighteen-month-old girl was shot as she sat on her father's lap in his car; and a nine-year-old boy was fatally wounded by a stray bullet as he sat at the dinner table drinking a glass of milk.

Events like these can make gang neighborhoods fearful places to live. When life is too dangerous on the streets, people stay in their homes with iron bars on their doors and windows to keep the violence out. Young people are afraid to go to schools where gang members roam the halls and hang out on the playgrounds. Children avoid parks and streets where gang members deal drugs and stage gun battles. People fear getting caught in gang violence even while shopping at local stores. Businesses in gang neighborhoods, too often subjected to gang-instigated burglary, theft, and extortion, struggle to survive.

The rise in violence is due, in part, to the avail-

A former gang member shows his scarred arm to a friend. Many of the injuries from gang violence are comparable to those seen in wartime.

ability of high-powered weapons. Today, gang members arm themselves with Uzis, AK-47 assault rifles, M-16 rifles, 9-mm semiautomatic pistols, and AR-15 semiautomatics.

"It used to be that you'd have fifty guys on a side who'd meet in a park at midnight and go at it," Sgt. Joe Guzman, a sheriff's gang expert, told the *Los Angeles Times*. "Today, instead of brawling, it's all about guns. It's all about firepower. It's all about taking people *out*."

Most of the weapons used by gang members were once viewed as weapons of war. In fact, the carnage caused by gangs with these weapons has turned some neighborhoods into virtual war zones. The Martin Luther King Jr./Drew Medical Center located in a gang-torn neighborhood in Los Angeles, even trains army doctors because the hospital frequently treats wounds normally seen only in war.

Non-drug-related violence

Many experts say the greatest percentage of gang violence is unrelated to drugs. Most gang violence is tied to revenge or erupts over challenges to reputation. An article in *Time* magazine in June 1990, reported: "Respect and disrespect make up the reigning ethos of the streets. Kids seek respect by joining a gang, they prove themselves by punishing someone outside the gang for an act of disrespect."

Disrespect or "dissing" in gang terminology, shows itself in various ways. In the world of gangs, a verbal insult, a rival gang member's presence in another gang's territory, or even wearing enemy colors constitutes disrespect and often provokes a violent response.

"In Los Angeles you can 'dis' a rival gang by uttering an irreverent nickname; 'cheese toes' is a slang word for Crips and a sure way of provoking a gun battle," one magazine reports.

Sometimes, crime and violence are ways gang members gain a reputation. Some gang members, especially younger ones, commit violent crimes to prove they are brave or dependable. One Los Angeles gang member told writer Bing: "In my set you get a rep by straight killin'."

Stealing for status

Violence may also be the result of a gang member's quest for expensive status items, such as jewelry or cars. A recent trend in gang violence is to commit a holdup or murder in which gang members steal a person's athletic shoes or sports team jacket. All across the United States, young people are being injured or killed for their clothing. "But, of course, these assailants aren't simply taking clothes from their victims. They are taking status," says a May 1990 *Sports Illustrated* article.

Chicago police report approximately fifty incidents involving jackets and about twelve involving shoes per month. Much of this crime is thought to be gang-related.

Still, other gang members shoot people for little or no reason. "These guys today, they're cold-blooded killers. Kill you for a shirt, a piece of chicken, a dirty look," said former New York police detective Steve Allie Collura.

Often, the murders are done in a drive-by shooting, in which gang members in a car drive up to members from another gang and spray them with bullets. One Los Angeles gang member told Bing how he shot and killed a member of an enemy set who was walking in his turf. The man's wife and baby were also injured in the shooting. The killer recalled:

> So I strapped it [an AK-47] to the seat . . . and we circled around and pulled up on this [guy] from two blocks away, crept up on him slow like, and I just gave it to him. . . . I lit his ass *up!* I killed him—shot his baby in the leg—crippled his wife! . . . She in a wheelchair now, I heard, wearin' a voicebox, 'cause one of the bullets caught her in the throat.

When Bing asked him why he did it, he said, "For all our dead homeboys. For bein' our enemy. For slippin' so bad."

One killing usually triggers another. If a gang member is injured or killed, his homeboys get re-

A shattered car window shows some of the aftermath of a drive-by shooting in Washington, D.C.

venge by killing a member of the gang who shot him. The gangs are then at war and the killing can go on for years.

In another gang battle, an eleven-year-old boy was shot to death in Los Angeles in April 1991. The accused killer showed no remorse. After the killing, he matter-of-factly told investigators: "The child shouldn't have been there. I was aiming for someone else."

Perhaps the most chilling aspect of gang violence is the attitude of gang members toward it. Killing has become a way of life, a game. "Big-city ghettos and barrios are full of teenagers whose poverty and deprivation have immunized them to both hope and fear. The result is a casual acceptance of—and sometimes enthusiasm for—torture and murder," *Newsweek* reported in 1988.

Some gang members view their own possible violent death as casually as they view the violence they inflict on others. Said one female member of the Los Angeles Crips: "I ain't afraid no more. I seen a lot of Crips die and it looks easy. It don't hurt to die. It kills you tryin' to stay alive here."

Drugs and violence

Though most fights are still fought for respect, reputation, and status, drugs are adding a new dimension to the violence in some areas. "The days when rival gangs fought each other only over turf and colors are fading fast. In Los Angeles, Chicago, New York and dozens of other cities, gang conflicts have become a form of urban-guerrilla warfare over drug trafficking," according to *Newsweek.*

Gangs deal in heroin, marijuana, PCP, hallucinogens, and especially, crack cocaine. Crack is cheap and highly addictive, so business tends to be steady. It is also lucrative. Some gangs earn as much as one million dollars a week selling crack.

With this much money at stake, gangs violently defend their sales territory. Drive-by shootings, payback killings, and murders over drug deals gone bad are common. "Informers, welshers and competitors are ruthlessly punished; many have been assassinated," *Newsweek* reported.

Other crimes

In addition to drug trafficking, gangs also make money through armed robbery, theft, burglary, and other crimes. Jewelry, guns, car parts, and electronic equipment are common bounty. These crimes can be committed by a group of gang members or by individuals who want to impress older gang members with their daring or earn money on their own. "I make money, but I don't hardly sell that much dope no more," one Los Angeles gang member told writer Bing. "I do jewelry licks. I go in jewelry stores, jack 'em up [hold them up], go sell the jewelry."

Chinese gangs are perhaps the most sophisticated money-makers on the gang scene today. They are especially noted for their extortion and protection rackets. They approach businesses in Asian communities and offer them protection against gangs—but for a price. Those who decline the offer frequently find their businesses targeted for violence. Police estimate that 80 to 90 percent of Chinese businesses in New York pay protection money to one or more gangs on a regular or occasional basis.

Deepening stress

Gang-related crime and violence take their toll on community residents in other ways, too. Psychiatrists, counselors, and others say thousands of children in gang-torn communities suffer from a form of posttraumatic stress disorder like that ex-

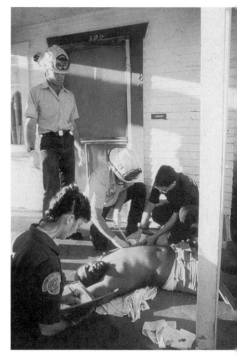

Paramedics work to save a drive-by shooting victim.

This woman complained to police about drug dealers outside her apartment. Later, gang members broke into her home and scalded her fifteen-month-old son.

perienced by some combat veterans.

Children who have witnessed gang warfare up close are often haunted by the sight, sound, and smell of gunfire. Psychiatrists Spencer Eth and Robert S. Pynoos report that children vividly remember a victim's screams or sudden silence, the splash of blood and human tissue, the gasp of a dying parent, and the eventual police sirens. Like combat veterans, these children experience nightmares and jitters and have difficulty sleeping.

With so much violence around them, residents of these communities often learn to live by gang rules. They adapt in order to survive. Robert Ferber, a member of the Los Angeles city attorney's gang unit, tells of one young man who sleeps on the floor instead of on his bed. He does this because he fears being killed in his sleep by stray bullets.

Nights can be difficult, but sunrise brings worries of another kind. Many parents in gang-populated neighborhoods urge their children not to wear gang colors to school. Children worry about not wearing them.

One young man, Ferber says, kept a stash of

clothes in his backyard. He wore the clothes his mother wanted him to wear when he stepped out the door but changed into gang colors for his walk to school. The young man was not in a gang. Nevertheless, gang colors offered some protection against beatings and losing his lunch money to gang members.

Schools also feel the tension of their neighborhoods. Some schools, according to Ferber, not only have fire drills and earthquake drills but drive-by drills as well. "The teacher blows a whistle and everybody falls to the ground."

In some cases, gang-related violence is so common that people just get used to it. Ferber recalled an interview he conducted with a middle-aged woman in a gang neighborhood. He asked her to describe how gangs had affected her life. She shrugged and said she knew of nothing that made her life different from anyone else's. For fifteen minutes, Ferber said, the woman tried to think of an incident, then, just as she was about to give up, she hit on something. "I guess," she said, "I could start with the day my daughter found the corpse in the garbage can."

In most areas, a corpse in a garbage can would be shocking and quite memorable. To this woman, however, it was so much a part of life, she had forgotten it. It was just another violent incident in a world filled with gunfire, helicopters, sirens, and death.

5

Solutions

AS DEATH COUNTS increase and whole neighborhoods slip into the gang world's grasp, people from all walks of life search for solutions. Most agree the key to success is cooperation. With that in mind, law enforcement officers, social workers, and citizens from battered communities have joined forces to find creative solutions to gang problems.

What these groups need most is accurate information. For a long time, statistics and data were hard to obtain. The National Youth Gang Project, established in 1987, tried to remedy that situation. The project's goal was to define the gang problem from a national perspective, find out what people were doing to solve gang problems, and try to determine which programs and policies are most effective in decreasing gang membership and violence.

The National Youth Gang Project found that community mobilization, the combining of forces and resources in gang areas, offered the best chance of success. They also discovered that in areas with chronic gang problems, finding jobs for young people and making sure they receive a good education are key factors in reclaiming gang youths and their neighborhoods.

Armed with this information, people have

(Opposite page) Father Gregory Boyle, who has tried to find solutions to Los Angeles gang problems, stands with boys from the gang-filled neighborhood where he worked.

63

taken action. Some groups hack away at the roots of the gang problem—poverty, discrimination, and hopelessness. Others work to get kids who are already in gangs out of them.

Social service agencies

Youth Guidance is an agency in Chicago that attacks the problem from many different angles. Founded in 1924 by Episcopal Charities, this privately funded organization offers schools a broad range of programs to help disadvantaged young people who live in the inner city. These services include individual, group, and family counseling; crisis intervention; creative arts programs; and job development and vocational education programs.

Louis Wright, a Youth Guidance gang prevention coordinator, works with young people at Harper High School in the Chicago neighborhood of West Englewood. West Englewood is a poor, predominantly African-American area where, according to Youth Guidance, "hopelessness has pervaded the community." The graduation rate at

Some communities are fighting to take back their neighborhoods. Here, a group of Muslim residents in Brooklyn prepares for a neighborhood patrol.

Harper High is only 42 percent, and the attendance rate is only 74.8 percent.

It is Wright's job to change these statistics. Along with John Ziegler, coordinator of Harper's drug-abuse program, Wright works with young people most likely to become involved in gangs. The program emphasizes prevention—keeping young people out of gangs—and intervention—getting them out of gangs once they join.

Wright contacts eighth-grade teachers and their students the summer before those students enter high school. He tries to find out which students are most likely to join gangs. Once he knows who the young people are, he visits them at home and gets to know them. He encourages them to enter programs that interest them. He tries to steer them toward a bright, productive future.

Students can take part in cultural awareness workshops, violence prevention classes, field trips, and athletic programs. Youth Guidance even sponsors a rap group whose music focuses on staying out of gangs, away from drugs, and in school. One program teams young men with older mentors to give them positive male role models.

"Our goal," says Wright, "is to expose them to positive people, places and things." This gives potential gang members options. It opens up new areas in which they can find success, and it helps build their self-esteem.

Some community members, tired of the crime in their neighborhood, have formed groups to discourage gang membership and violence.

Grass-roots organizations

Along with social service agencies, grass-roots organizations have sprung up in several cities. Some deal specifically with gang problems, while others address larger social problems that ultimately lead to gang activity. In the Watts neighborhood in Los Angeles, gang activity is particularly heavy. Parents of Watts is a group that tries to solve some of that community's problems.

Parents of Watts was founded in the early 1980s when a group of teenagers set fire to a car near Alice Harris's home. It took Harris three days to have the car moved. It took her about the same amount of time to quit her job and start working to solve the problems in her community.

Poverty is the primary problem in the community of Watts. Five low-income housing projects surround the neighborhood. Gang violence is high, and the streets can be dangerous.

"They say Watts is the core of trouble," Harris claims. "But anybody knows the core of anything is the best part—if we make it the best." So, along with other neighborhood residents, Sweet Alice, as she is known, decided to make Watts the best community it could be.

Community involvement

Though the group does not focus exclusively on gangs and gang-related problems, it has several programs designed to reduce gang membership and gang activity in the neighborhood. Parents of Watts runs a private high school for gang members and others and provides summer jobs for some of the school's students. These students earn money by cleaning up the community, doing yard work for senior citizens, and working in the Parents of Watts office. This work helps cultivate self-esteem in these young people.

Parents of Watts has helped 123 area students get into colleges nationwide and runs a home for students who attend college in the area. Harris says this home provides a safe and inexpensive living environment for young people who want to continue their studies but cannot live at home. In addition, Parents of Watts runs various other programs.

Members of Parents of Watts act as liaisons with government agencies, police departments, and social service organizations. Their common goal is to create a safe and thriving neighborhood. Only in this way, Harris says, by offering young people better living conditions, education, and hope for the future can anyone strike at the heart of the gang problem.

Individual efforts

Like Alice Harris, Father Gregory Boyle is an individual who has made a difference. In six years as priest at the Dolores Mission Church in Los Angeles, he focused primarily on gangs. He has tried to fill the gaps left by schools under siege, families under stress, indifferent or hostile employers, and underfunded social services. Boyle has become father, employer, teacher, and counselor to many gang members in the neighborhood.

Boyle's task has not been easy. The parish is the poorest in the Catholic archdiocese of Los Angeles, and there are from eight to twelve gangs that war in its two square miles. Between 1986 and 1992, Boyle buried twenty-six young people killed during gang violence

In the midst of this urban war, Boyle's solu-

Boyle, center, helped provide gang members with the support and acceptance they often lacked at home. Boyle developed personal realtionships with gang members and their families by visiting them in their neighborhood.

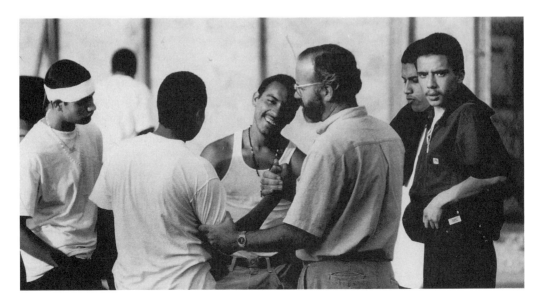

Helping gang members find jobs has been a priority for Boyle. Here, Boyle gives a haircut to a young man preparing for a job interview.

tions have been surprisingly simple. He offered young people what few others have been able to—jobs, an education, a safe place to talk, and someone to talk to.

When asked what he thinks will solve gang problems, Boyle says: "Jobs, jobs and more jobs." Then, he adds, "On a more lofty level love and care."

He helped gang members find jobs, even to the point of buying their clothes and cutting their hair for interviews. If local businesses would not hire them, Boyle employed them himself through his Jobs for a Future program. Funded by Boyle, the program employs gang members to work in construction, maintenance, and warehousing jobs. Some young people work in offices. One gang has even put together a gardening crew, subsidized by Boyle, that works for individuals.

Acknowledging the link between lack of education and gang involvement, Boyle and the other priests in his parish opened the Dolores Mission Alternative, a junior and senior high school for gang members.

Community groups

Boyle also helped form a community group called the Comite Pro Paz en el Barrio (the Committee for Peace in the Barrio). This organization views young gang members as the children of the community, not the enemy. Recently, they conducted a campaign to disarm their children by taking away their weapons.

Even with all the programs aimed at getting people out of gangs, perhaps the most important thing Boyle has done is treat gang members like people. He knows their names, takes an interest in their problems, and quite often has provided the acceptance and discipline they lack at home. Gang members have high praise for Boyle. He "is always there when you need him," one ex-gang member told the *Los Angeles Times Magazine* in 1991.

> I don't have a dad. So I think of him like my father. Even when I was in jail, he always had time to talk to me. Even when nobody else was there for me. And, you know, when I wanted to stop gang-banging, sometimes I would have so much anger that I wanted to do something, kill somebody. But I would talk to Father Greg and he would help me so I didn't explode inside. He's the one we can all look up to.

Boyle's six-year stint as pastor of the parish ended in July 1992. His departure came at a time when warring gangs in different parts of Los Angeles were trying to establish truces and abide by them.

In his final sermon Boyle spoke of his deep feelings for the young men and women whose lives have become so intertwined with gangs. He expressed anguish over the violence that forced him to bury so many gang members and pleaded for them to make peace between themselves and their communities. "The gangbanging must stop. Please make it stop," Boyle said. "If you do that then I will know that you love me."

Law enforcement

In the war against gangs, law enforcement officers are on the front lines. In the past, police departments could find no way to deal with gang problems without using force. They arrested gang members and put them in jail. Even though these tactics got some gang members off the streets, they did little to solve the problems. Those arrested were eventually released, and younger boys were still joining gangs at a rapid pace.

"Force hasn't worked," said Yolanda Chavez, liaison between the Los Angeles mayor and the city's Latino community. "Police harassment

A member of a police department anti-gang unit takes part in a massive sweep against suspected gang members.

Individuals are getting involved to help make a difference in their communities. Here, actor Edward James Olmos urges a crowd of nearly 150 gang members to end gang violence in Los Angeles.

hasn't worked. Jail and Juvenile Hall hasn't worked. Without options, gangs will thrive."

So in many gang communities, law enforcement agencies are beginning to work together with other groups. They are still arresting and jailing gang members, but they are also helping community organizations to get and keep young people out of gangs.

For example, in January 1991, sheriff's officials met with leaders from thirty-five Los Angeles communities. They decided to combat gangs by focusing on social problems. Their proposed plan of action included removing graffiti from city walls, developing counseling services for families, testing young people for learning disabilities, and ridding parks and schools of gang members.

"This workshop is a first step in getting every community in the county to work together with law enforcement and on the same wavelength," said Steve Valdivia, executive director of Community Youth Gang Services.

Drastic measures

In some areas, city officials and law enforcement officers are trying more drastic measures to solve the problems. Early in 1990, police barricaded streets in a notorious gang neighborhood in Los Angeles. They erected wrought-iron roadblocks that they hoped would reduce drive-by shootings and help area residents feel safer. Since the installation of the barricades, police have reported a 67 percent drop in drive-by shootings and a 10 percent reduction in street crime.

In addition, police officers on bicycles were assigned to the neighborhood. They went door-to-door, getting to know the residents. They told parents about athletic and academic programs open to young people.

"It is like what you would see in the movies; a

cop walking up and down the street, getting to know the neighbors, and listening to your problems. I enjoy it. I really do," one area resident said. Others, however, said they felt like prisoners. "We are not living over there in South Africa, so why close us in?" one person asked.

Things everyone can do

Whether a person lives far away from areas where there are gangs or in the heart of a gang neighborhood, there are many things he or she can do to help solve the problems. Everyone can get involved.

For example, the problems of poverty and discrimination are national. No matter where a person lives, he or she can find out what local politicians are doing about these problems. A young person can write to elected leaders, take part in existing volunteer programs, or work to create new ones.

On a more personal level, individuals can fight personal prejudices by learning to appreciate cultural and ethnic differences. Within their communities and families, young people can speak out against racist remarks and practices.

Young people who are being pressured to join a gang can search for alternatives—a sports organization, an arts program, school activities, or a church group. They can also ask for help from people like those in Parents of Watts and Youth Guidance.

These young people can do a lot on their own, but they also need help from adults inside and outside of their communities. Programs and organizations must be available so that they have somewhere to turn for help. Accomplishing this will require a more complete understanding of the problems and greater effort and cooperation in finding creative solutions.

Glossary

barrio: A low- or moderate-income, Spanish-speaking neighborhood.

basehead: A crack addict.

clique: A gang group whose members are roughly the same age or have similar interests.

club: A branch of a larger gang.

crack: A highly addictive, inexpensive form of cocaine.

dime speed: A gang term for a ten-speed bicycle.

dissing: A gang term that means to show disrespect.

gangbanging: A gang term that means either street fighting or just hanging out with other gang members.

graffiti: The inscriptions made by gang members on walls and signs.

homeboy/homegirl/homie: A gang member.

jumped in: An initiation rite in which a prospective member is beaten up before being allowed into a gang.

jumped out: A ritual beating imposed on gang members who wish to leave a gang.

lit up: A gang term that means to be shot.

nowhere: A gang term that refers to a youth who has no gang affiliation.

placas: Graffiti or a personal signature used in graffiti.

representing: Showing outward signs of gang affiliation, such as wearing gang colors or tattoos.

rumble: Once common gang slang for "street fight."

set: A small, independent gang that takes the name of a larger gang to share its reputation.

vatos: Gang slang for "guys."

Suggestions for Further Reading

Herbert Asbury, *The Gangs of New York*. New York: Blue Ribbon, 1939.

Leon Bing, *Do or Die*. New York: HarperCollins, 1991.

Celeste Fremon, "Father Boyle and the Homeboys," *Los Angeles Times Magazine*, August 11, 1991.

James Haskins, *Street Gangs Yesterday and Today*. New York: Hastings, 1974.

Vincent Riccio, *All the Way Down*. New York: Simon, 1962.

Rick Telander, "Senseless," *Sports Illustrated*, May 14, 1990.

David Wilkerson, *The Cross and the Switchblade.* Bernard Geis Associates, 1963.

Works Consulted

Leon Bing, "When You're a Crip (or a Blood)," *Harper's Magazine*, March 1989.

Montgomery Brower, "Gang Violence: Color It Real," *People Weekly*, May 2, 1988.

Lorenzo Carcaterra, "Color Them Deadly," *Gallery*, November 1988.

Janice Castro, "In the Brutal World of L.A.'s Toughest Gangs," *Time*, March 16, 1992.

Nina J. Easton, "Everyplace Enemies of the Family," *Los Angeles Times*, March 1, 1992.

FBI Law Enforcement Bulletin, "Gang Behavior: Psychological and Law Enforcement Implications," February 1983.

S. C. Gwynne, "Up from the Streets," *Time*, April 30, 1990.

George Hackett, Nonny Abbott, Michael A. Lerner, and Frank S. Washington, "The Drug Gangs," *Newsweek*, March 28, 1988.

Berkley Hudson, "Children Increasingly Fall Victim to Gang Violence," *Los Angeles Times*, October 26, 1991.

C. Ronald Huff, ed., *Gangs in America*. Newbury Park, CA: Sage, 1990.

David R. Johnson, *Policing the Urban Underworld*. Philadelphia: Temple University Press, 1979.

Susan Kuczka, "County Police Want to Regain High-Tech Advantage on Gangs," *Chicago Tribune*, November 28, 1991.

Joan W. Moore, *Homeboys*. Philadelphia: Temple University Press, 1978.

Dean E. Murphy, "Barricades, Police Visits Give Hope to Crime-Plagued Neighborhood," *Los Angeles Times*, June 22, 1991.

Jacob A. Riis, *The Battle with the Slum.* Montclair, NJ: Patterson Smith, 1969.

Louis Sahagun, "Sheriff's Officials, Community Leaders Shift Gang Strategy," *Los Angeles Times*, January 16, 1991.

Martin Sanchez-Jankowski, *Islands in the Street: Gangs in American Urban Society*. Berkeley: University of California Press, 1991.

Luc Sante, *Low Life: Lures and Snares of Old New York.* New York: Farrar, Straus & Giroux, 1991.

Ronald L. Soble, "Community Contact Vital to Curbing Gang Violence, Police Told," *Los Angeles Times*, July 3, 1991.

Irving R. Spergel et al., "National Youth Gang Suppression and Intervention Program," unpublished paper, University of Chicago, 1990.

Del Stover, "A New Breed of Youth Gang Is on the Prowl and a Bigger Threat Than Ever," *The American School Board Journal*, August 1986.

Jerry Thomas, "Teen Tells of Gang's Brutal Sendoff," *Chicago Tribune*, December 11, 1991.

U.S. Office of Juvenile Justice and Delinquency Prevention, "National Youth Gang Suppression and Intervention Program," Washington, DC: Juvenile Justice Clearinghouse, 1991.

James Diego Vigil, *Barrio Gangs*. Austin: University of Texas, 1988.

Tracy Wilkinson and Stephanie Chavez, "Elaborate Death Rites of Gangs," *Los Angeles Times*, March 2, 1992.

Index

About the Author

Karen Osman is a free-lance writer whose published works include numerous plays and short stories for young people, humor, and nonfiction articles. She has a bachelor's and a master's degree in theater. When Osman is not writing, she directs cross-cultural plays. She currently lives in the southern United States.

Picture Credits